JK's
Quick Start Guide
to Scrivener (Mac)

Other books in JK's Self-Publishing Guides:

eBooks

JK's Quick Start Guide to Scrivener (Windows)

JK's Quick Start Guide to Publishing Books on Amazon KDP

JK's Quick Start Guide to Amazon Ads Marketing

JK's Quick Start Guide to Publishing Books on Ingram Spark

JK's Quick Start Guide to Copyrighting Your Book

JK's
Quick Start Guide
to Scrivener (Mac)

JK Lincoln

ISBN 978-1-938322-59-4

Ralston Store Publishing
P.O. Box 1684
Prescott, Arizona 86302

Table of Contents

Note   1

Before We Begin   2

Step-by-Step Instructions   4

Appendix A   55

Appendix B   60

Author's Note   69

Other Books   70

Note: The following two pictures depict the same thing. The two arrows point to the same part of the window *Assign Section Layouts*. But please notice that the content of the pictures is slightly different. You may find as you go through the lessons that what you see on your screen and what you see in the lessons are different. There are different versions of Scrivener with slight differences. But the arrows and the text in the lessons will always show you exactly what to do.

i. Before we begin, the next two pictures may or may not come up. If you see this, click *Choose Backup Folder* and then choose one. Documents is a good choice, unless you already have a special folder for your writing.

Choose Backup Folder

Scrivener can back up your projects automatically whenever you close a project. Please choose a folder for automatic backups below.

Choose Backup Folder...

/Users/test89etc./Documents

You can change this setting at any time via the Preferences panel (available from the "Scrivener" menu).

Next

ii. You can choose to take the tutorial. It is always available to you and will teach you a lot of if you take the time to read it. Click *Start Using Scrivener* so we can begin.

Take Tutorial?

If you're a new user, the easiest way to get up and running is to take the interactive tutorial. The tutorial is itself a Scrivener project, so you use and learn the software at the same time.

You can access this tutorial at any time from the "Help" menu.

Take the Interactive Tutorial Now

Start Using Scrivener

1A. When you open Scrivener for the first time, this is the screen you will see. All the options are available.

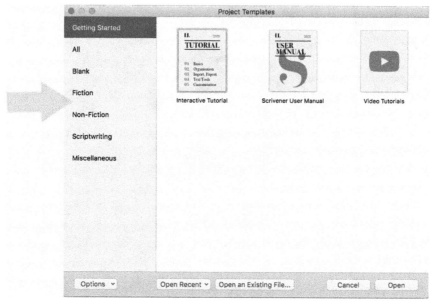

1B. When you choose an option, it will highlight it in blue. In this lesson, we will choose *Fiction* and *Novel*. Click on both *Fiction* and *Novel* so they're highlighted and then click *Choose*. (Even when I write non-fiction, I still choose *Fiction* and *Novel*. It seems easier to work with.)

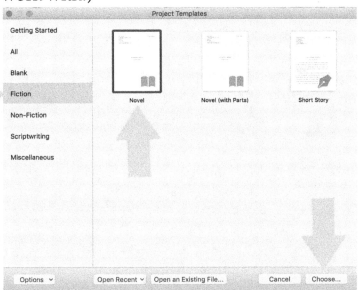

2A. The new little window that pops up will have "Untitled" in the *Save As* box. Name your new project and then choose where to save it. (You can ignore *Tags*.) In the picture, this project will be saved in the *Documents* folder. Click *Create* at the bottom right-hand corner of the new window.

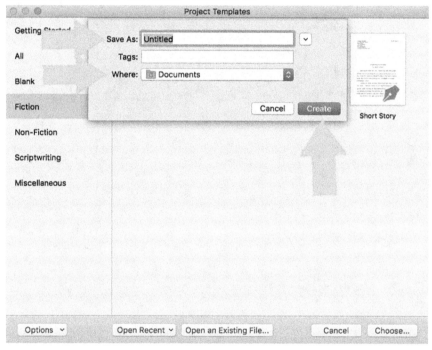

2B. This may pop up. You choose.

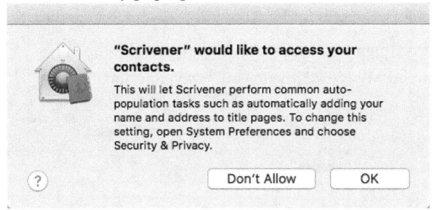

2C. This may pop up next. If you know how to move your document, click *Show Project in Finder* and move it now. Then proceed to 3. Otherwise, click *Show Project in Finder and* continue with 2D.

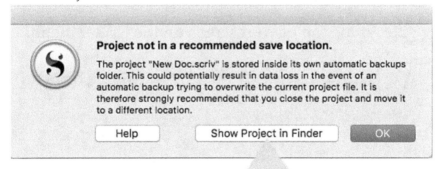

2D. Your window should look similar to this. It is the *Documents* folder. You will probably have other documents in yours. The document with the big **S** titled My New Novel is my Scrivener document .

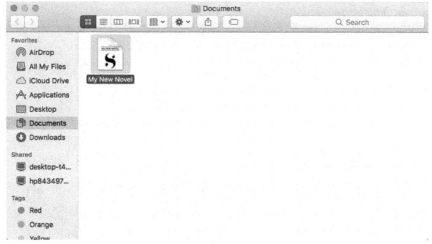

2E. At the top of your screen on the Finder menu, click *File*.

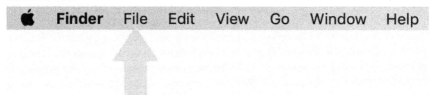

2F. On the dropdown menu, click *New Folder*.

🍎 **Finder**	**File**	Edit	View	Go	Window	Help

New Finder Window	⌘N
New Folder	⇧⌘N
New Folder with Selection	⌃⌘N
New Smart Folder	
New Tab	⌘T
Open	⌘O
Open With	▶
Print	⌘P
Close Window	⌘W
Get Info	⌘I
Rename	
Compress	
Duplicate	⌘D
Make Alias	⌃⌘A
Quick Look	⌘Y
Show Original	⌃⌥⌘A
Add to Dock	⌃⇧⌘T
Move to Trash	⌘⌫
Eject	⌘E
Find	⌘F

● ● ● ● ● ● ●

Tags...

2G. Now you can see the new folder. See how *untitled folder* is blue? It's ready for you to type in the new name. Then tap the Enter or Return key.

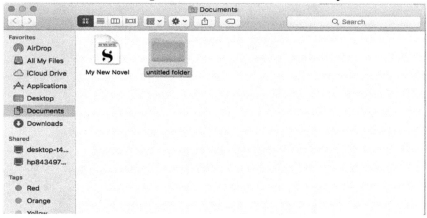

2H. I named mine *My New Novel*. Now drag the Scrivener document into your new folder using click and drag. The white one with the big **S** is the document. If the document disappears, you were successful. It means it's now in the new folder you created.

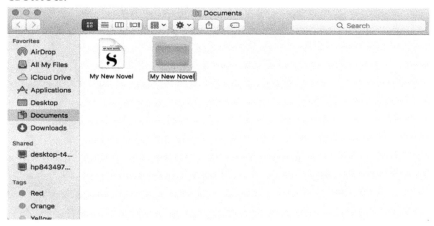

2I. To get back to Scrivener, go to your Dock. This is a picture of the right side of my Dock. Yours may look different, but it will have that big white S, which is the Scrivener icon. The little black dot beneath it means that it's an active program. Click on the icon now to continue.

3.This is the screen you will see next. You will learn a lot if you read this page, but to get you started, move on to number 4A. (You can always come back to this page by clicking *Novel Format* or *Non-Fiction Format* on the top of the list on the left.)

****

NOTE: If you plan to import your manuscript from Word, please go to Appendix B at this time.

****

4A. Click on *Chapter*. It will now be highlighted.

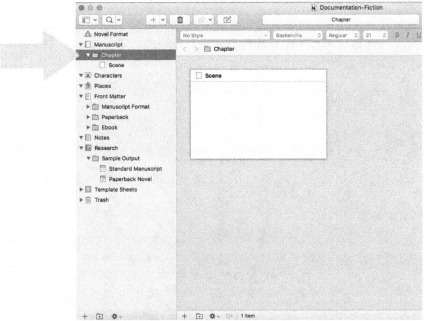

4B. At the top, there is a small + with a downward "arrow" right next to it. Click and HOLD the arrow to get the *New Folder* option to pop up. Click on *New Folder*.

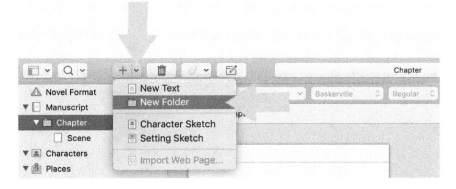

4C. It will create a new folder at the same "level" as the one called *Chapter.* Whenever you want to create a new folder, you must have a folder at the same level highlighted. Type in Chapter One.

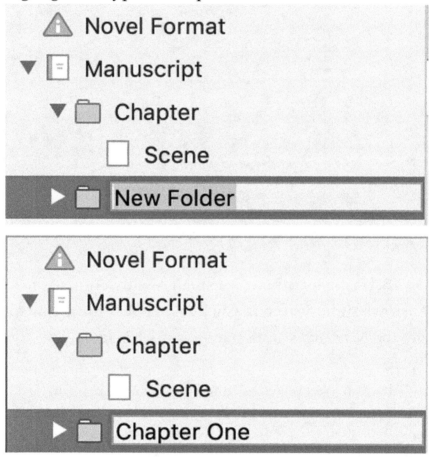

4D. After you type in Chapter One, tap the Enter or Return key on your computer. It will then look like this.

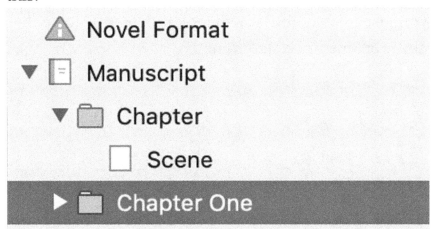

5A. Now, return to the + at the top of your screen. This time we will click the + NOT the downward arrow. It will create a sub-document *inside* the folder you just created, (but it will look indented.) Name the new document. I called mine *1*.

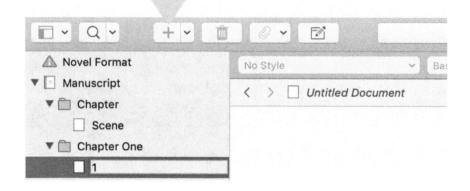

5B. And then tap the Enter or Return key to make it look like this. It should be indented from your folder named *Chapter One*.

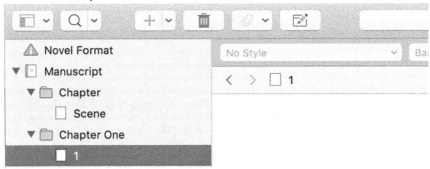

That is the difference between creating a folder and creating a document inside the folder. Hold down the downward arrow to get the *New Folder* option to pop up for a folder; and click the + to create a new document—just be sure to first click and highlight the folder where you want to put the document.

5C. Now click on *Chapter One* and then proceed to the downward arrow to use the *New Folder* pop-up option to create another new folder. Call it Chapter Two and tap *Enter* or *Return* to make it so.

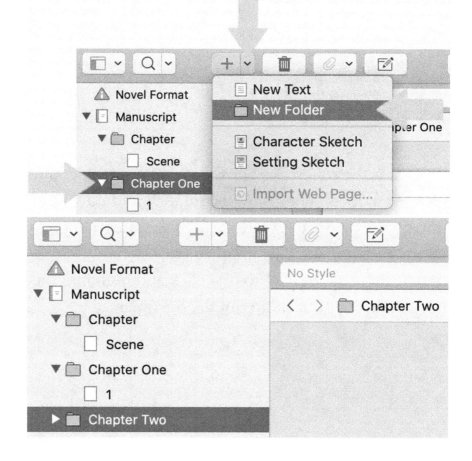

5D. Now click on the + again to create a new document inside *Chapter Two* called 2 and tap *Enter* or *Return*.

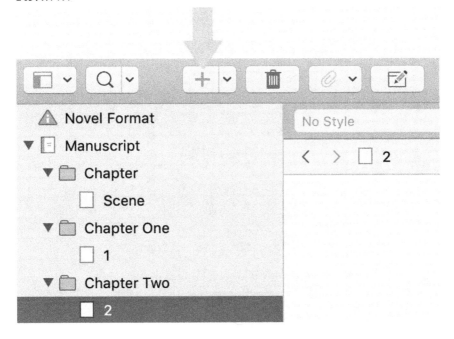

5E. Follow 5C and 5D to create a *Chapter Three* folder and a *3* document. To make sure that the *Chapter Three* folder is beneath the *Chapter Two* folder, be sure to click *Chapter Two* before you create the new folder. (Although you can always drag it to where it belongs if you make a mistake.)

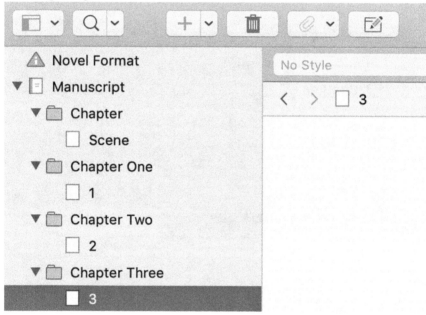

5F. Now click on the 1 under *Chapter One*. It will highlight it. Then click in the white area on the right. A blinking cursor will appear in the upper left corner of the window, and the *1* on the left will become shaded instead of highlighted.

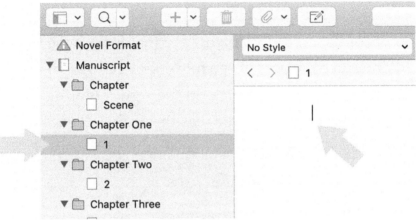

5G. Voila! That's it! Start typing!

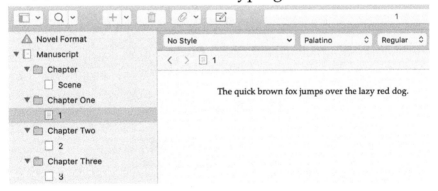

6. Something necessary to complete before starting *Compile* is the *Front Matter*. It is on the left-hand side of the screen, somewhere under the last document you just created.

Inside the Front Matter folder (you can tell the other folders and documents are inside because they are indented), you will see folders for *Manuscript, Paperback,* and *Ebook*. Click on the right pointing arrows on *Paperback* and *Ebook* to see this. Please note that *Ebook* doesn't have as many options as *Paperback*.

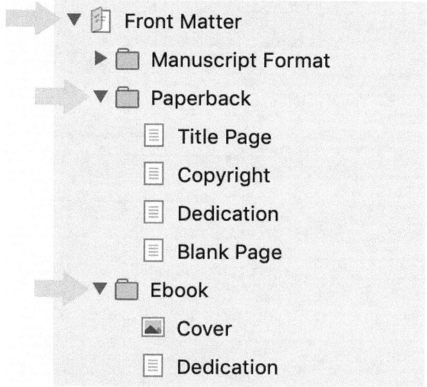

You can add more options (like "Other books") by following the instructions on numbers 4 and 5 above. You do not need to use the pages they provide. I always substitute my own copyright page to make it how I like it. (You can also change it.) Your copyright page for paperback and eBook will be different, because eBooks don't always need an ISBN number. When they do need one, it will be different from your paperback. I don't include a cover anymore because Amazon puts it in for me, but whether or not you include your cover in the eBook file, you need to delete the placeholder cover under *Ebook* (by dragging it into the trash) AND EMPTY THE TRASH!!! If you don't, the placeholder pic keeps showing up in places you don't want it to show! It's very persistent! Drag the *Cover* file into the *Trash* now. (The *Trash* is at the bottom of the list on the left. You may have to scroll to reach it.)

Quick lesson on emptying the trash. For those who already know how, proceed to the next page.

Q-1. At the top Scrivener menu bar, click *Project* and then click *Empty Trash* on the new menu that pops up.

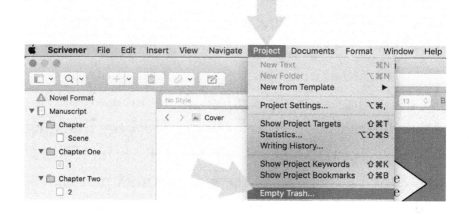

Q-2. This little window pops up. Click *OK*.

Q-3. Now that you can see the trash is empty (because nothing is beneath it), proceed to 7A.

Now the most difficult part of the program: the *Compile* feature. But don't worry, I've made it easy. People have written entire books on just this process alone, so please understand that I will only give you one way to do it that will work. There are many ways.

7A. On the right side of the Scrivener menu bar, you will see this icon. The little box beneath it where it says *Compile for export or print* shows up when you mouse over the icon. Click the icon now.

7B. The next window that pops up depends on two things: The big arrow points to *Print*. There are other choices including PDF and eBook. The small arrow points to *Formats*. If you had chosen *Non-Fiction*, these would be slightly different. The process remains the same, though.

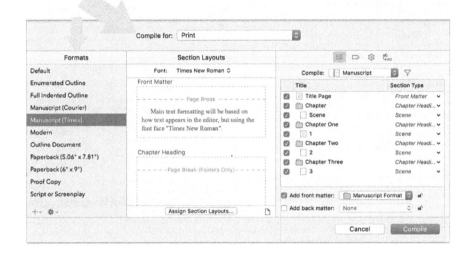

7C. Now the fun begins! First click where it says *Paperback (6" x 9")*. We will copy that format. Don't worry if your book is not that size. You will have the option of changing it later. Then click on the + at the bottom left and choose *Duplicate & Edit Format*. (Even if your book is 6 x 9, you need to make the changes I describe here.)

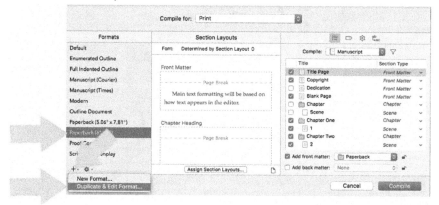

7D. See where it says *Paperback (6"x9") Copy* beside *Format Name*? Now is the time to change that to whatever you want. If you are going to change the size, you probably want to reflect that size here. Where my right-hand arrow is, click on the button for the drop-down box and choose *My Formats* beside the *Save To* option. That will make sure it saves to the right place and will always be available.

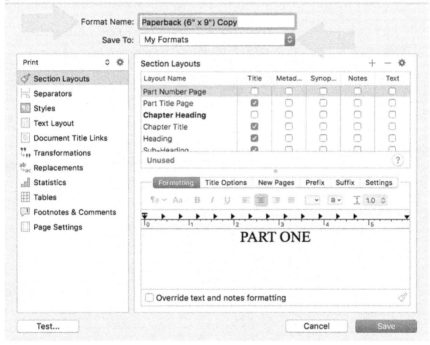

7E. After changing the name and the *Save to* option, click *Page Settings* on the bottom left-hand side of the window.

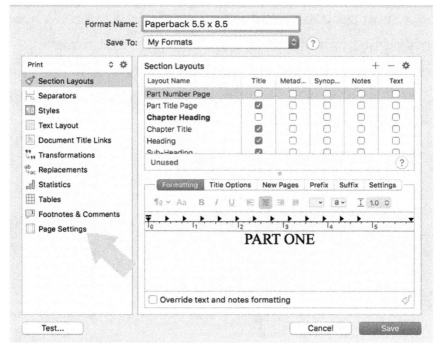

7F. Notice that everything on the right-hand side has changed. Up near the top, click on *Page Setup*. This is your chance to change the size of your book.

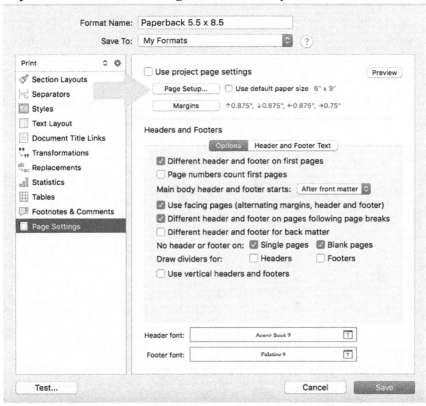

7G. A small window will pop up. Please note that beneath the *Paper Size* box, it says *6.00 by 9.00 inches*.

Page Setup
Page Attributes ⌄
Format For: Any Printer ⌄
Paper Size: Other ⌄
6.00 by 9.00 inches
Orientation: [⬆] [⬆]
Scale: 100%
? Cancel OK

7H. Now click on the drop-down box for *Paper Size*.

Page Setup
Page Attributes ⌄
Format For: Any Printer ⌄
Paper Size: Other ⌄
6.00 by 9.00 inches
Orientation: [⬆] [⬆]
Scale: 100%
? Cancel OK

7I. A list of different sizes will pop up. If the one you want is there, click it. Otherwise, click *Manage Custom Sizes... .*

7J. This is the screen you'll see—unless a new size has already been created. Click on the +.

Paper Size:	0 in	0 in
	Width	Height

Non-Printable Area:

User Defined

	0 in	
0 in	Top	0 in
Left	0 in	Right
	Bottom	

+ — Duplicate

? Cancel OK

7K. Fill in the correct width and height that you want it to be. Leave the *Non-Printable Area* alone.

Page Setup

Untitled

Paper Size:	5.5 in	8.5
	Width	Height

Non-Printable Area:

User Defined

	.25 in	
.25 in	Top	.25 in
Left	.56 in	Right
	Bottom	

+ — Duplicate

? Cancel OK

7L. Look in the striped box on the left. First, click on the highlighted *Untitled*, then click on it again so it looks like the center picture which will allow you to change it. Then change it to something more identifiable—like the size. Tap the *Enter* or *Return* key.

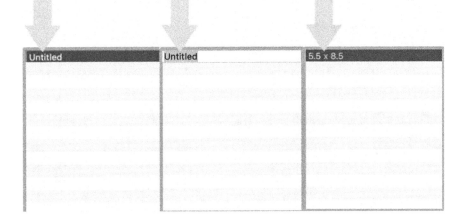

7M. The entire window will look like this afterwards. Click *OK*.

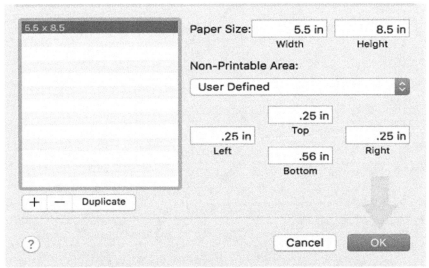

7N. Now under *Paper Size,* you can see it has been changed to what you entered in the previous screen. Click *OK.*

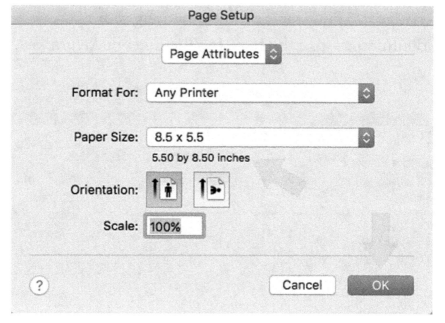

8A. Now go back to the top of the left-hand list and click *Section Layouts*. Then look at the center part of the screen that also says *Section Layouts*. There are checks on various items under *Title* and *Text*. You may have to scroll down to see everything in that little portion of the window. Erase ALL CHECKS EVERYWHERE EXCEPT these three under the *Text* column: *Chapter with Title* (NOT Chapter Title), *Table of Contents*, and *New Page*.

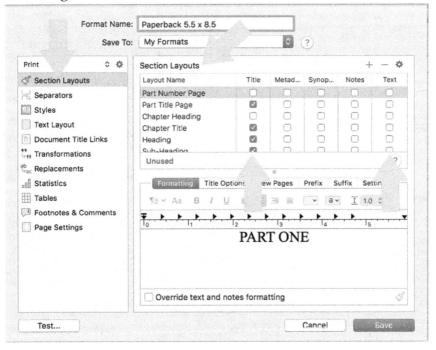

8B. It should now look like this. Nothing is checked except *Chapter with Title, Table of Contents,* and *New Page*—all under the *Text* column only.

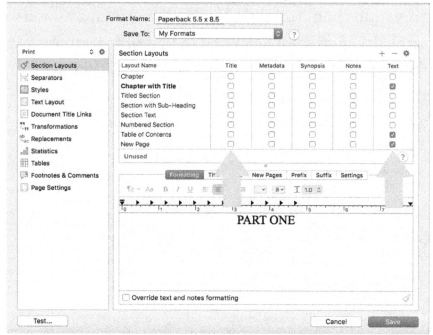

8C. Click on *Chapter with Title* and then click on *New Pages* (second arrow) on the center menu bar. Then Change the numbers for the third and fourth arrow to whatever you want. *Pad top of page* refers to a new chapter starting partway down the page. I usually leave it at 8. *Number of opening words to make uppercase* is also for a new chapter. I usually use 3 or 4 for that. Now click *Save*.

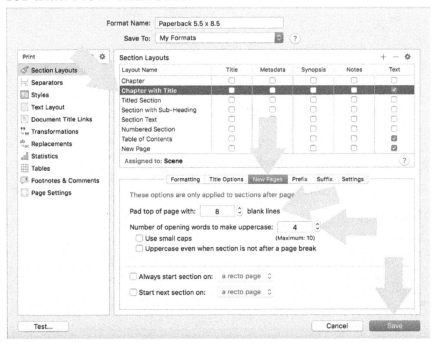

9A. Now click where it says *Assign Section Layouts* at the bottom of the center section.

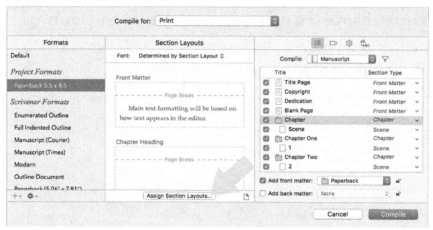

9B. On the left-hand side under *Section Types*, click or make sure that *Chapter Heading* is highlighted. In the center section under *Choose layout for "Chapter Heading" documents*, scroll down until you get to *As-is*, then click on it or make sure it's highlighted.

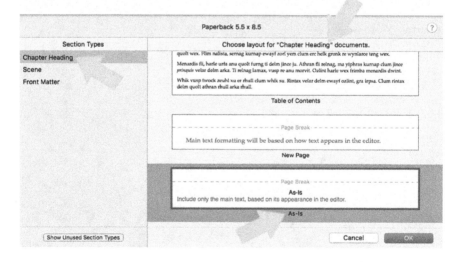

9C. On the left-hand side under *Section Types*, click *Scene*. In the center section under *Choose layout for "Scene" documents*, click on *Chapter with Title*. (You will probably have to scroll up.) If you did choose Non-Fiction instead of Fiction, this will be *Section* instead of *Scene*.

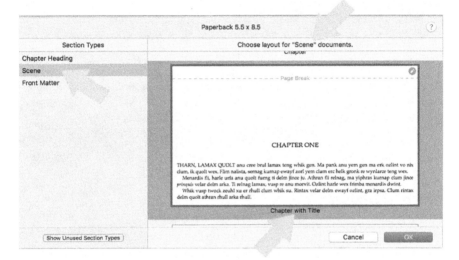

9D. On the left-hand side under *Section Types*, click *Front Matter*. In the center section under *Choose layout for "Front Matter" documents*, click on *As-is*.

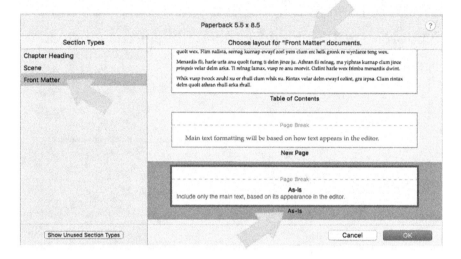

9E. If you click on the bottom of the left-hand side where it says *Show Unused Section Types,* you will see . . .

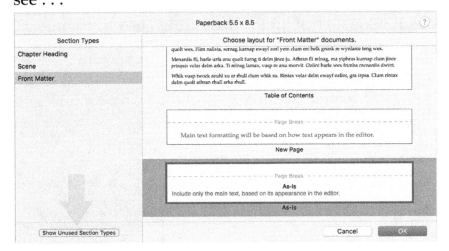

. . . the unused section types. Click the Hide button in the same place if you want to hide them again. Then click OK.

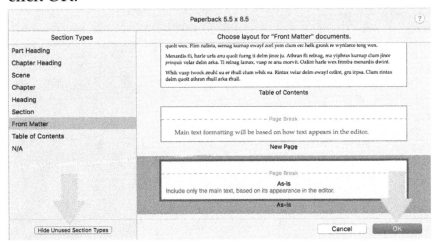

10A. Note that underneath the little box on the right side of the window, there may or may not be a check where it says *Add front matter*. IF you're working on an eBook, click on the drop-down box to change it.

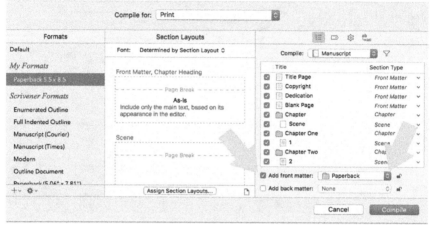

10B. Just click on *Ebook* to change it. Depending on what you choose, the list above the *Add front matter* box will change.

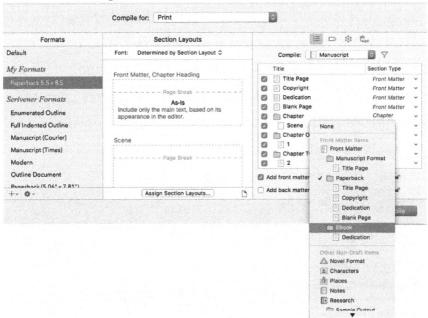

10C. After choosing *Paperback* or *Ebook*—for the *front matter*—it will bring you back to this screen. Before you compile (AFTER your book is written), make sure everything you want and nothing you don't want has checks under the arrow. You can see that I have unchecked where it says *Dedication,* *Chapter,* and *Scene.* For me, I usually use that Scene file (and more added to it) to put comments about places, characters, and future books. Regardless, it doesn't belong in the compile for this book.

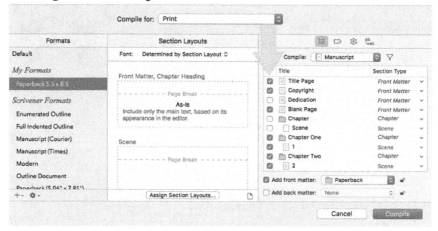

11A. Almost done. Do you want a print book or an eBook or something else? Click the downward arrow.

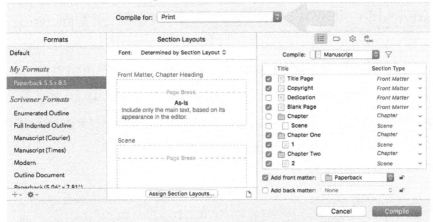

11B. For paperback, I choose *Print* and then take the PDF option. That way, I can see what the book looks like first. If you choose *PDF*, it just saves it as PDF without giving you a chance to look. (Although you can always look later, it's more convenient to look now.) For eBooks, sometimes I choose .epub and sometimes I choose .mobi. Amazon KDP accepts both. We'll leave it *Print* right now.

✓ Print
PDF

Rich Text (.rtf)
Rich Text with Attachments (.rtfd)
Microsoft Word (.docx)
Microsoft Word 97-2004 (.doc)
OpenOffice (.odt)

Plain Text (.txt)
Web Page (.html)

Final Draft (.fdx)
Fountain Screenplay (.fountain)

ePub Ebook (.epub)
Kindle Ebook (.mobi)

MultiMarkdown
MultiMarkdown → LaTeX (.tex)
MultiMarkdown → OpenOffice (.odt)
MultiMarkdown → Web Page (.html)
MultiMarkdown → Flat XML (.fodt)

12A. One last thing before you do the compile. Up at the top of the window, click the second icon that looks like a tag. If you pass your mouse over it, it will say *Set metadata such as title and author.*

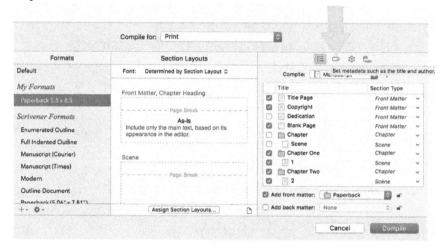

12B. This is the screen that will pop up next. Fill in the title and author EXACTLY how you want it to appear. (On my title that you see, there is more to the title than shows.) It doesn't matter what you put in the *Abbreviated Title* field.

Title:	JK's Quick Start Guide to Scrive
Abbreviated Title:	Quick Start Scrivener Mac
Authors:	JK Lincoln
Forename:	JK
Surname:	Lincoln

Cancel   Compile

12C. If you want to get back to the other screen for one last check, click the icon that looks like a list.

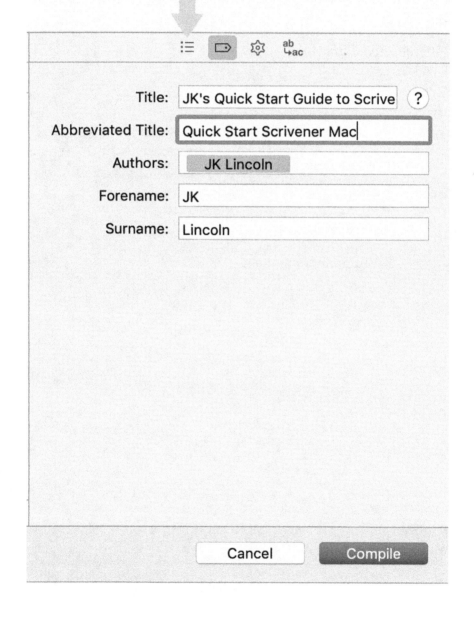

12D. NOW you can click *Compile*!

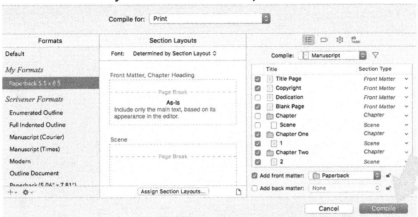

.

APPENDIX A
If You Don't Have Scrivener Yet

Appendix A-1. Go to the Scrivener website, which is: https://www.literatureandlatte.com. Choose to either *Buy Now* or to *Download Free Trial*.

Appendix A-2. This is the *Buy Now* screen. $49 is an incredible price for a program like this. And no, I don't get any kind of a commission, I just really think it's a great program. If you choose to buy it, click the *Buy Now* button and follow the prompts for payment and download information.

Appendix A-3. This is the Download Free Trial screen. If you choose the *Free Trial,* click the *Download* button and follow the prompts.

Appendix A-4. Skipping ahead to the point where you're ready to open the program. If it doesn't automatically open, go to *Go* on the *Apple Menu,* choose*Applications*, and then click *Scrivener* to open it.

	Finder	File	Edit	View	Go	Window	Help

Back ⌘[
Forward ⌘]
Select Startup Disk on Desktop ⇧⌘↑

Recents ⇧⌘F
Documents ⇧⌘O
Desktop ⇧⌘D
Downloads ⌥⌘L
Home ⇧⌘H
Computer ⇧⌘C
AirDrop ⇧⌘R
Network ⇧⌘K
iCloud Drive ⇧⌘I
Applications ⇧⌘A
Utilities ⇧⌘U

Recent Folders ▶

Go to Folder... ⇧⌘G
Connect to Server... ⌘K

Appendix A-5. This pops up. If you only want the Free Trial, click *Try* and then skip to Appendix A-6. If you are ready to buy, click *Enter License*. Underneath the two arrows, it says *Scrivener will stop working after 30 days of use unless you buy a license.*

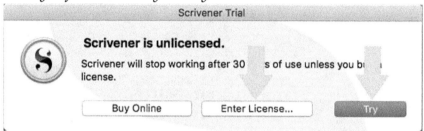

Appendix A-6. Enter the name you signed up with and the serial number they gave you. Then click *Register*.

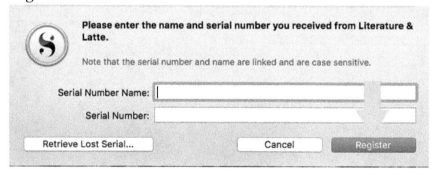

Appendix A-7. This may or may not pop up. I would highly recommend clicking the *Check Automatically* option. When it pops up to let you know there is an update available, you can always click on *Remind me later*.

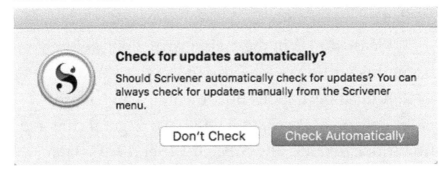

Now is the time to return to the main book, section i to continue your lessons.

APPENDIX B
How to Import your Word Document into Scrivener

Before we begin:

1. Please do 1-3 in the main instructions before you begin this portion of the import.

2. It must be a *.docx document. If you have an older version of Word, you will have to get it changed from *.doc to docx. How? See if a friend has a later version of Word. Or you can do a search for a free online converter. It's simple. You upload your *.doc and download the newly converted *.docx.

3. If your document has chapters, and you want Scrivener to recognize them, then you need some kind of "separator" to tell Scrivener where your chapters are. If your chapters are labeled Chapter One, Chapter Two, Chapter Three, etc., then you can use "Chapter" as you're separator. However, if, as you were writing you used "Chapter One . . . CHAPTER TWO . . . 3 . . . Four," then you will have to change them to something uniform. If your chapters are just labeled with numbers or they have names instead of numbers, then you can put a # (or $ or @ or whatever) at the end of the chapter to designate a separation. (If you choose

not to do this, you can still import, but you will have to separate the chapters by hand.) Regardless, you will probably have to do some tweaking after it's imported.

Appendix B-1. First, click on Manuscript.

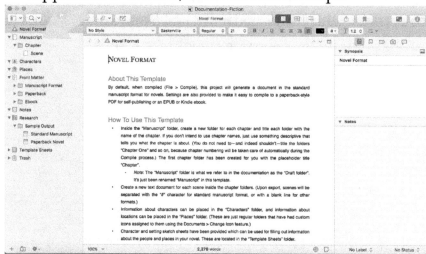

This is what the screen will look like now:

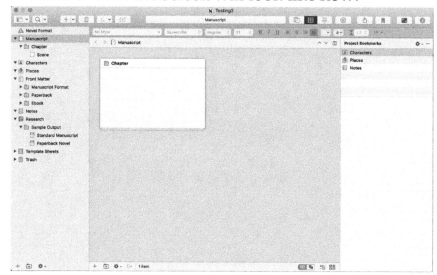

Appendix B-2. From the dropdown menu at the top, choose *File, Import,* and *Import and Split*.

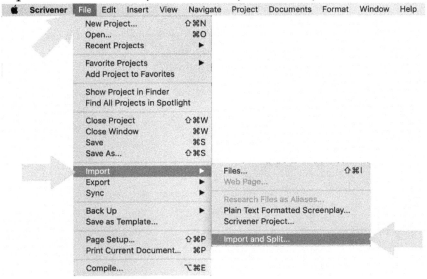

Appendix B-3. This is what comes up next. You can see where I typed in CHAPTER in the *Sections are separated by*: section.

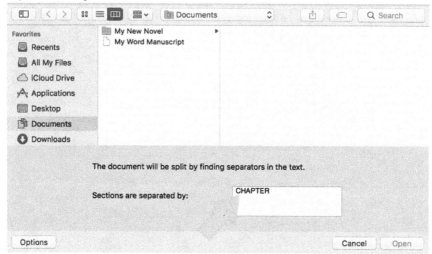

Or you can use a "pound sign" or "hashtag" or a $ or % or anything you choose. But if your chapters are labeled "Chapter," that's the easiest. And remember that case matters. If your chapters are CHAPTER, but you put Chapter in that box, you'll get one big, long chapter. (And if that happens or some other mistake, you can always drag the file/s into the trash, empty the trash, and try again.) Dragging it to the trash does not affect your original document. Still, you should always always ALWAYS have another copy of your manuscript.

The document will be split by finding separators in the text.

Sections are separated by: #

Options   Cancel   Import

Appendix B-4. Choose your Word document and then click *Import*.

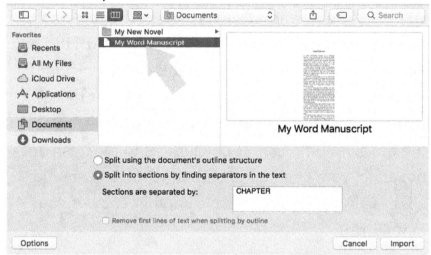

Appendix B-5. This is roughly what you'll see next on the left-hand side of your window. It all depends on what you chose as your separator and how you formatted your manuscript. And as I said before, you will probably need to tweak it.

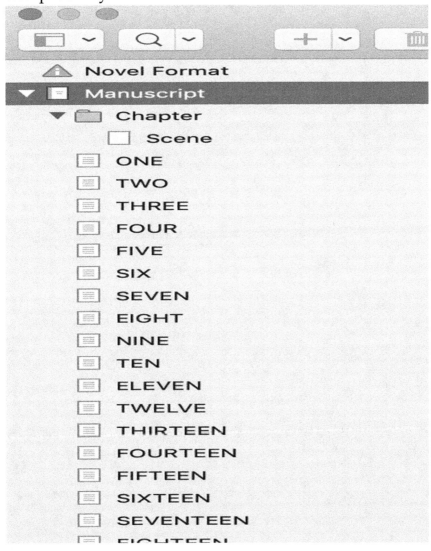

Now, please continue with 4A on page 13 to get the real feel of this awesome software.

Author's Note

If you have any questions or comments about one of my Quick Start Guides, please ask or comment on my blog:

https://self-publisherquickstartblog.blogspot.com.

Also, write in if you have any requests for a new Quick Start Guide. Thank you!

If this book helped you and you liked it, please leave a review on Amazon or Goodreads. I would appreciate it.

Thank you!

Other books published by Ralston Store Publishing:

Time Travel Sweet Romance
Cowgirls in Time Series by Erica Einhorn
A Chill Wind
Wind Beneath My Wings
Against the Wind
The Healing Wind
Ride Like the Wind
Wind of Change
The Way the Wind Blows

Rutledge Historical Society Cozy Mysteries
Message for Murder
Death over Divorce
Kousins Kan't Kill
Rogues to Riches
Secrets for Sale
Lady Smith Lady

Children's Books
Sparkles the Unicorn and Kindness
Cooper's Smile
The Little Unicorn Who Could
Do Bears Poop in the Woods?
Can Pigs Fly?
Why Do Puppy Dogs Have Cold Noses?
The Invisible Lion
La Petite Licorne Qui Pouvait
Das Kleine Einhorn Was Es Kann
The Little Unicorn Who Could Coloring Book
Do Bears Poop in the Woods? Coloring Book

Caregiving
The Journey that Matters by Jodie Lightener

Suspense
Darkness in the Light by J.K. Lincoln

India
Not My Guru by Parvati Hill

Women's Fiction/Reincarnation
Two Lifetimes, One Love by Thea Thaxton

Yoga Books
Bathroom Yoga
Airplane Yoga
Wheelchair Yoga
Essential Yoga on Horseback
Exercises for Therapeutic Riding

www.ingramcontent.com/pod-product-compliance
Lightning Source LLC
LaVergne TN
LVHW052311060326
832902LV00021B/3818